Facts About The We

By Lisa

Facts for Kids Picture Books by Lisa Strattin

Eurasian Eagle Owl, Vol 44

Eurasian Lynx, Vol 45

Zebra Finch, Vol 46

Golden Finch, Vol 47

Purple Finch, Vol 48

Yellow Finch, Vol 49

Poison Dart Frogs, Vol 50

African Dwarf Frogs, Vol 51

Prairie Falcon, Vol 52

Vermillion Flycatcher, Vol 53

Sign Up for New Release Emails Here

http://lisastrattin.com/subscribe-here

All information in this book has been carefully researched and checked for factual accuracy. However, the author and publisher makes no warranty, express or implied, that the information contained herein is appropriate for every individual, situation or purpose and assume no responsibility for errors or omissions. The reader assumes the risk and full responsibility for all actions, and the author will not be held responsible for any loss or damage, whether consequential, incidental, special or otherwise, that may result from the information presented in this book.

I have relied on my own observations as well as many different sources for this book and I have done my best to check facts and give credit where it is due. In the event that any material is used without proper permission, please contact me so that the oversight can be corrected.

Table of Contents

INTRODUCTION

Western Lowland Gorillas are declared an endangered species. It is one of two species of the large ape group but the number of population of this one is more than their near relatives, the Mountain Gorillas. The gorilla population is found in the Maiombe Forest that covers a large tract of Cabinda, Democratic Republic of Congo and Republic of Congo. They have also been found in Ebo / Ndokbou (Cameroon) where their exact number is unknown. They choose to live in heavy rain forests. Western Lowland Gorillas tend to be a bit smaller in size than their mountain cousins. They also have shorter hair and longer arms.

COLOR ME

CHARACTERISTICS

Gorillas live around trees and can easily climb them. They frequently roam on the ground in groups having as many as thirty gorillas in a group. Their flocks are systematized and they follow mesmerizing social structures. Their groups are mostly led by one principal, aging adult male who is known as a silverback because of the ribbon of silver hair that beautifies his otherwise dark fur showing its age and contributing to the group through his experience. These groups have a varied number of several other young males, females and young ones.

COLOR ME

The Western Lowland Gorilla is the largest of all apes. Their shoulders are wide and broad. They have a muscular neck and their hands and feet are very strong. Their significant size allows them to defend themselves against any expected attack by   predators. They live in relative protection on the ground, more so than any other primate. Their body is sheltered by short, thin grey-black or brown-black hair but its face has no hair, they do have a thick ridge of hair above their eyes very much like the eyebrows of human beings. They can cover short distances with two legs but prefer to largely get around by walking on all fours. While walking on all fours they walk on their knuckles, not their open hands.

COLOR ME

DIET

They eat both meat and plants by nature; nevertheless, they are occasionally classified as herbivores because they do love to feed on plants and live chiefly on fruits, leaves and shrubbery. They sometimes supplement their diets with insects such as termites and ants. They usually do not drink water because they are able to get sufficient moisture from the foliage they consume. A gorillas diet is alike to that of the chimpanzee.

COLOR ME

Yet, these gorillas eat bigger fruits as well as mature leaves and twigs. About 67% of their diet is fruit, 17% is comprised of seeds, leaves, stems etc. The rest of their diet includes insects, including termites, caterpillars and other insect larvae. They eat fruits during the rainy season and feed on enough herbs and bark in the dry season. When fed in captivity they preferred eating vegetables, fruits and leaves. Gorillas in captivity incline to eat less bulk food than those in the wild. An adult male gorilla eats about 60 – 70 pounds of food per day but the adult female gorillas eat about two thirds of that amount.

COLOR ME

LIFE STAGES

A gorilla gets sexually mature between the ages of 7 to 8 when it is found in a wild whereas in captivity it attains sexuality when it is nearly 5 and 1/2 years old. Gestation period of a female lasts from eight to nine months. In the wild, female gorillas typically deliver their first babies when they are 10 – 11 years old. Usually they give birth to a single baby gorilla each time. After the delivery of the baby gorilla, the mother gorilla cuts the umbilical cord herself.

COLOR ME

At the time of birth, infant gorillas weigh around 3 – 5 pounds and have light hair jacket covering their pink-grey skin. The mother gorilla embraces her infant belly-to-belly for close contact until it gets strong to hang onto her hair at about 2 months of age. A father who is usually a silverback pays a role of patient father and plays with the baby once it grows into a "toddler" age baby. The crawling of infant gorillas begins when it is about nine to 10 weeks old. It starts walking on its all four limbs.

COLOR ME

The white patch on the body of an infant helps the mother to keep a track of the baby and also supports other group members in recognizing the fact that it is a baby. The rear patch begins to vanish at about three years of age. Weaning is also done by mother at this stage. Females leave the group when they attain an age of 8 or 9 years; afterwards they join an unrelated group or a lonely male. Males remain with their natural group until they are about 12 years old. They start leaving the group whenever they wish. Solitary males attempt to get the attention of females from other groups to form their own group.

COLOR ME

The occurrence and extent of breeding in gorillas are low in contrast to the other great chimps. Only the silverback, or leading male, is allowed to mate with the adult females in the group. The success of males to find mates depends upon the protection of exclusive rights of the adult females, which is protected by males forming an undying bond with each female in a social group. The formation of these protections keeps adult females away from leaving the group or breeding with other males.

COLOR ME

LIFE SPAN

Western Lowland Gorillas live around 30 to 40 years when reared in the wild and 40 to 60 years when kept in captivity.

SIZE

Male height ranges from 5 to 5 1/2 feet and the female height ranges from 4 to 4 1/2 feet. An average male weighs around 350 to 400 pounds and an average female weighs around 200 to 225 pounds.

COLOR ME

FRIENDS

They live in groups and become their own friends. The only potential killers to the Western Lowland Gorilla are leopards and human beings.

COLOR ME

For more Kindle Downloads Visit Lisa Strattin Author Page on Amazon Author Central

http://amazon.com/author/lisastrattin

To see upcoming titles, visit my website at LisaStrattin.com – all books available on kindle!

WESTERN LOWLAND GORILLA PLUSH

You can get one by copying and pasting this link into your browser: **http://amzn.to/1tjLqGn**

Printed in Great Britain
by Amazon